Sutherland
Down Memory Lane
A pictorial history

Sutherland – down memory lane

ISBN: 978-1-907323-06-5

We would like to acknowledge and thank Willie Morrison, formerly of Durness, for providing many of the photographs within this book and for all the help he gave in its production.

ESTABLISHED
1899

Produced by the Northern Times, Main Street, Golspie, Sutherland KW10 6SA.
01408 633993

Dolina Ross from Achlyness and Peter Jack from Forres, whose descendants in British Columbia, Canada, still hark wistfully at the thought of Achlyness as their spiritual home, although Dolina's father Robert, who moved there with his parents in the mid-19th Century, was the second last child to be born on the island of Handa. The couple married in 1911 and a few months later Peter, a plasterer and decorator, emigrated to Vancouver to seek a better life for himself and his new bride. Dolly and their two-year old son Bobby, who was born at Achlyness, followed in 1914. Bobby never returned to his birthplace, but his son Peter scattered his ashes at the bottom of the family croft, after his death in 1992.

A group pictured at Achlyness in the late 1920s. The man with bonnet may be Angus Corbett, Portlovorachie, and the chap on the left is probably Willie Falconer.

Achlyness school and pupils, with teacher Barbara Mackay, a native of Overscaig, on Loch Shin-side, where her parents were tenants of the popular fishing and staging hotel. She married in 1938, a minister, the Rev Tom Donn, then incumbent at Rosehall, Sutherland, and eventually moved to Inverness, where she died in 1999.

Recently qualified civil engineer Alan Sutherland on a motorcycle, with an unidentified friend on the pillion, pictured outside Sutherland County roads department offices, Brora, around 1930. Alan, born in Paisley in 1906, and brought up in Renfrew, returned in 1928 to the county from which his ancestors had been evicted several generations before, to work as a junior roads engineer for three years, before moving on to Ross and Cromarty and later to England. He finished his career in 1971 as the Scottish Development Department's chief engineer for the Crofting Counties, based in Edinburgh, but retained a deep love of Brora, and especially its golf course, until his death in 1987

Inchnadamph Sunday School picnic, August 1930, taken at Ardmair, near Ullapool.

Another photo from the 1930s, taken at Achlyness. Curstag Ross who died in 1982 at the age of 92 is on the left; Alec John Corbett is at the right; the man at rear is Hector Ross, Curstag's brother, who also died a nonagenarian. The girl at front may be Mary Falconer

Alan Sutherland (1906-87), then a junior roads engineer with Sutherland County Council, took this dramatic photograph of flooding at Kintradwell, north of Brora, in 1931. This area was beset by a series of serious floods in the late 1920s and early 1930s

Colin Campbell, from Sangomore, Durness, served his time as a blacksmith at the family forge, but spent much of his working life as handyman at Cape Wrath Hotel, Keodale – hence the salmon. He was also well known for obliging local men, living as they did 60 miles from the nearest barber, by cutting their hair. Though he never sought a fee, clients by gentlemen's agreement, generally slipped him a packet of cigarettes. Smoker nonetheless, he lived until well into his nineties

Angus Mackay (Pongo) and Jackie Macpherson (right), pictured at Laid, Durness, in the late 1940s. Bachelor Pongo, who lived with his sister, was a popular local character, and believed to have been the last exponent of a very local step-dance called the puirt-nam-bagh.

Sisters-in-law Alex and Lizzie Munro, pictured at their home at Hilton, Dornoch, in December 1961. The two ladies were celebrated for their great hospitality. Lizzie's husband and Alex's brother Jackie, who died in 1959, was a local coal merchant, who also owned a substantial croft. After his death Alex and Lizzie were landladies to a small and very privileged band of youngsters from North West Sutherland who attended Dornoch Academy.

Ardmore School pupils, late 1930s.

Ardmore Side School pupils c1930.

Bonar Bridge School mid 1930s.

This photo was taken by a travelling photographer at Sangobeg, Durness, around 1908. The children are from left: Kate Morrison, later known as Ceat Mhor or big Kate, to distinguish her from a younger sister also named Catherine, is pictured here with her oldest sister, Johann, and twin brothers George and Donald Morrison, wearing frocks, as little boys of two or three, then often did. The twins were born in September 1905. Their father David was a local crofter and lobster fisherman, who like many of his contemporaries also pursued a trade, in his case, a shoemaker.

Third-year pupils pictured at Dornoch Academy in 1956. They are, rear row, from left: Hamish Leslie, Lindsay Robertson, both Dornoch; Neil MacConnell, Bonar Bridge; Alex Dingwall, Spinningdale; Willie Morrison, Durness; Ken Fraser, Embo; middle row, from left: George Gunn, Melness; Joe Brinklow, Ospisdale; Maris Macdonald, Spinningdale; Margaret Mackay, Bonar Bridge; Leonard Will, Dornoch; Alaistair Mackay, Bettyhill; front row, from left: Susan Lindsay, Dornoch; Anne Paterson, Bonar Bridge; Rhoda Mackay, Kinlochbervie; Sheena Mackay, Anna Ross, both Embo; Ann Ross, Dornoch; Giorsal Campbell, Tongue; Marigold Mackenzie, Lochinver.

A carefree group by the boundary wall at Dornoch Academy, pictured shortly before the end of summer term,1959. They are, from left: Rhoda Mackay, Kinlochbervie; Jan Cowan, Dornoch; Norma Milne, Bonar Bridge; Lindsay Robertson, Dornoch; Alaistair Mackay, Bettyhill; Kenny Greig, Lairg; Frankie Carmichael, Dornoch; Giorsal Campbell, Tongue; Maris Macdonald, Spinningdale; Marigold Mackenzie, Lochinver. Photo from Jessie Sutherland, nee Grant

This happy group was snapped outside Dornoch Academy in 1959, again shortly before the end of the summer term. They are, rear, from left: Rhoda Mackay, Kinlochbervie; Agnes Morrison, Kinlochmore; Marigold Mackenzie, Christina Macaskill, both Lochinver; Evelyn Robertson, Dornoch; front, from left: Susan Lindsay, Dornoch; Lilian Mackenzie, Stoer; Jessie Joan Grant, Embo, now Jessie Sutherland, who contributed this photo.

These young ladies living at Ross House Hostel, Dornoch, then residential accommodation for secondary-age girls from rural Sutherland, attending Dornoch Academy, were photographed in 1956. Those in the picture are, rear row, from left: Mary Munro, Tongue; Nancy Mackenzie, Stronchrubie, Assynt; Betty Mackay, Talmine; Ann Macleod, Stoer; Ann Munro, Droman, Kinlochbervie; Elizabeth Mackay, Scullomie, Tongue; Joan Ironside, Kinlochbervie; Donnella Mackay, Allt-na-Suileag, Reay Forest; Giorsal Campbell, Tongue; Jean Macdonald, Ben Loyal Lodge; third row, standing, from left: Sandra Mackay, Scourie; Janette Douglas, Halladale; Chrissie Sutherland, Helmsdale; Janet Mackenzie, Drumbeg; Anne Macleod, Grumbeg, Altnaharra; Janice Macleod, Stoer; Barbara Mackay, Sheigra; Doris Mackenzie, Bettyhill; Fiona Grant, Stoer; Rhoda Mackay, Kinlochbervie; Georgine Maclean, Stoer; Margaret Morrison, Durness; Pamela Bowker, Tongue; second row, sitting, from left: Anne Mackay, Scourie; Janet Macaskill, Fanagmore; Ruby Munro, Durness; Elizabeth Mackay, Lairg; Joyce Macleod, Tarbet; Marsaili, Melness; Agnes Morrison, Kinlochmore; Marie Mackay, Bettyhill; Christine Gunn, Skerray; Ray Anderson, Stronchrubie, Assynt; Lilian Mackenzie, Stoer; Iris Mather, Durness; front row, kneeling, from left: Babette Mackay, Kirtomy; Rachel Gillies, Tongue; Marie Mackenzie, Lochinver; Marie Gillies, tongue; Catherine Matheson, Merkland; Jessie Mackay, Strathnaver; Marigold Mackenzie, Lochinver; Maureen Mackenzie, Tongue. Photo lent by Iris Mackay, nee Mather.

13

Dolly Macdougall, photographed with children of Durness Primary School Gaelic Choir at Brora, 1967.

Donald and Mina Corbett 1950s. Donald, from Kinlochbervie, and Williamina Ross, from Achlyness, married in 1910, and spent the remainder of their lives at Inchnadamph, where he died in 1960, and she in 1965. He started work there in late Victorian times, as a coachman at Inchnadamph Hotel, retraining as a chauffeur-mechanic, with the advent of the motor-car. He was still working part-time at the hotel, in his beloved workshop, on the day before his death.

Dornoch Academy teachers, photographed outside the "Old Academy" in the early 1960s.

Popular Tongue merchant Gordon Burr, second from right, front row, was fear-n-tighe at this Durness Christmas Concert in 1968. Sitting beside him is George Campbell, then the local county councillor for Durness, in the faraway days when Britain's most north-westerly mainland corner still enjoyed indigenous representation in the corridors of local government.

Cape Wrath Hotel – Jessie Macpherson, Ina Sutherland, and two others unknown.

Durness, blacksmith Hugh Campbell, photographed near his Sangomore home, probably in the 1920s, when the village boasted at least two smiddies.

Elderly widow Ellen Mackay, pictured outside her cottage at Achins, Durness, probably in the 1920s. The cottage has long since been demolished, and Ellen many decades dead, but several descendants still live in Inverness, including her grand-daughter, Joyce Morrison, from whom this photo came.

The children of Durness Primary School 1948, photographed shortly after the beginning of the autumn term.

Durness crofter-fishermen, pictured at Rispond in the 1890s.

Inchnadamph Wedding – late 1930s.

Matheson Wedding.

This photo shows a scene from a vanished ritual - the annual gathering by local crofters for the communal sheep-clipping at Smoo fanks in Durness in 1967, The rather worried looking fellow in the middle is George Morrison, Sangobeg, who died in 1989, while the slim young fellow at the left with the cigarette is his nephew, John Donald Sutherland - still a successful crofter, but now with a rather more substantial shadow. Between them, with the beanie cap is Angie Morrison, the local joiner. The young man on the right is Billy Campbell, who followed in his father's footsteps as the local builder, while beside him, with the bonnet is John "Brivard" Campbell, now the community's oldest man, but currently in care in Elgin. The communal clipping, all done by hand, is no more, with electric shears having replaced the manual instruments, although the fanks are still used for communal dipping.

Another photo from the communal fanks at Durness, 1967. Among those in the photo are the late Tommy Macleod, kneeling down, his father, second from right, Davie Mackenzie, right, and Ian James Campbell, the lanky teenager, now long-since a grandfather. Can anyone identify the wee boy on the left of the photo?

Durness crofter and local Great War naval hero Henry Macdonald, is pictured at the oars of a boat, just off Durness, along with relatives, around 1950. Sitting on the gunwale, left, is Henry's brother-in-law Albert Skinner, while at the stern is his sister, Robina Skinner. The young lady next to Albert is Peggy Macdonald, Henry's third daughter, while the little girl between Albert and Robina is his youngest daughter, Joan, who contributed this photo. Like many heroes, Henry, who won the Distinguished Service Medal in an action in the Dardanelles, would speak about the incident, although Joan says she understands that the officer leading the action, thought to have been an early commando-style raid on Turkish artillery batteries, won the Victoria Cross.

Inchnadamph - Two maids on the old bridge.

Pictured here in all their finery, about the turn of last century, are six of Kinlochbervie crofter Lachlan Ross's 11 daughters. Standing, from left, are Lexie, who emigrated to New Zealand; Mina, who made her home in York; Lucy, who went to London; Katie, who finished up a few miles from home at Polin; front, from left: Ina, who lived in London, and Chrissie, who also went to New Zealand. Lachlan, who was known as "Lachlan County", also had five sons, one of whom, Norman, was killed in the Great War.

The boys of Earls Cross Hostel, taken in 1954, five years after it opened as a residential facility for young lads from rural areas of Sutherland continuing their secondary schooling at Dornoch Academy. The hostel closed in 1992, made redundant after the establishment of senior secondary schools at Bettyhill, Kinlochbervie and Ullapool.

Inchnadamph School – Teacher Ruby Corbett with, from left, James Mackenzie, Margaret Mackenzie, Annella Morrison (in front), John Mackenzie and Charlie MacCuish. Ruby is still alive, aged 92, and the children are all now in middle age (July 2009).

The Melness Band from the late 1950s with (from left) Joseph Mackay, Donnie Campbell, Bally Mackay and Willie John Barnetson. Willie John is now (2009) the only survivor of what was a very popular and musical quartet. This photo was contributed by Donnie's son John, who now owns a garage in Lairg.

Pupils at Melness School around 1949.

Durness Post Wagon at Rhiconich Hotel, circa 1906. The driver and owner is Robbie Morrison from Durness, who held the mail contract for many years and later bought a Ford Model T, after receiving a modest inheritance from the estate of a relative abroad. Known as Robbie the Post, he was sometimes a little too sociable, and lost the contract, in the course of a drinking session, after revealing to mine host at Rhiconich Hotel the sum he had tendered. The latter latter later bid successfully for the mail contract, but he too received his come-uppance when the Kinlochbervie Estate, which owned the hotel, changed hands, and the new proprietor, a teetotaller, insisted on banning the serving of drink. Soon afterwards, the building became a police station, which it remains to this day.

This quintet was pictured in Scourie, around 1930. They are Isy Thomson, John Mackenzie, unknown, Marion Mackenzie and Ainslie Thomson

A charming study from the 1940s of twins Sandra and Donald Mackintosh at Rhuvoult, Kinlochbervie.

The Mackay family of Lerin, Durness, early 1900s. At the front is local crofter and tailor Edward Mackay, his youngest son Danny, who was killed at the Somme during the Great War, and his wife Flora Macdonald, a cousin of "Bobo" Macdonald, who became the Queen's nanny. Standing from left are daughter Jane, son John who married Hughina, son George, who later lived in Sangobeg, daughter Mary and son James. Contributed by James's grand-daughter Christine MacCormick, now living in Bearsden, but still the owner of the family house in Lerin, Durness.

Dornoch Academy Primary School circa 1949. Rear, from left: Sandy Thomson, Hamish Leslie, (thought to be) Willie Gow, George Sinclair, Sandy George; third row, from left: Peter Doull, Willie Wickham, Sandy Mackay, Ian Ligertwood, Willie Melville, Colin Macrae, Neil Macdonald, Archie Macrae, Gordon Currie; second row, from left: Isobel Gillanders, Marion Shearer, Dolly Gow, Ella Matheson, Minnie Mackay, Violet Murray Flora Macdonald, Catherine Campbell, Ann Melville, Ruth Munro, Kathleen King; front row, from left: Florrie Grant, Kathleen Leslie, Barbara Kennedy, Nancy Macdonald, Rena Mackay, Rosina Leslie, Sheana Maclean, Irene Murray, Frances Philips, Jean Begg, Catherine Mackenzie. This photo was contributed by Kathleen Leslie, now Kath Brown, of Brora.

Sutherland SWRI Federation meeting in the mid-seventies.

Golspie Cubs in the mid-sixties - Back row (left to right) - Kay Melville (Akela), David Duncan, Alan Weir, Robert Mackay, John Fraser, James Yuill, James Miller, David Baddon, Dorothy Mackay. Second row - Neil Buchanan, Alastair Grant, Alister Mackay, Alexander MacManus, Alastair Joyce, Sandy Mackay, Don Dickson. Front row - Rosas Urquhart, Ken Houston, Michael Baddon, Robert Mackay, David Polson, Alan Mackenzie.

Brora Concert Party in the mid-seventies at the High School assembly hall..

Golspie teachers at a first aid course in the mid-seventies.

Golspie Red Cross detachment 1977. Back row – Margaret Jack, Barbara Cumming, Irene Brown. Middle row – George Ross, Nancy Grant, Marie Macleod, Bunty Robertson, Blanche Sinclair, Kay Murray, John Turney. Front row – Barbara Inkster, Etta Manson, Roddy Cameron, Elsie Mackay, Olive Weir.

Lairg Primary School Gaelic Choir with headmaster, William H Campbell, in 1978.

Golspie SWRI..

Ardgay brothers and sister John, Peter and Katie Williamson, snapped at Inchnadamph on their last sortie to West Sutherland with their pony and cart in 1978. The Williamson family were popular with crofting folk in North and West Sutherland, where in days before the motor car they brought items of domestic ware, haberdashery and news. They lived in a spotless cottage in Ardgay for most of the year, latterly only venturing out at the height of summer. When the trio departed a campsite, the only evidence of their occupation was a slight flattening of the grass where their bender had been – unlike today's travellers, who so often abandon their rubbish wherever they decide to camp, and then quote human rights when locals complain.

Wali Mohammed, pictured at Durness, in the early 1990s. Wali came from Pakistan to Wick in the late 1950s, and set up in business as an itinerant trader, travelling around North West Sutherland in his van. He also had a shop in Wick, where he settled for many years, and raised a family, but despite prospering considerably, continued to make personal visits to long-term clients until he moved to Inverness, some years after this photo was taken. A well respected and popular man, he was also very dutiful about attending funerals of many of the friends he made.

In March 1978, Mrs Violet Henderson of Tower Street walked out with a trolley full of groceries as one of the lucky first customers at the village's modernised Co-op grocery store in Main street. Also pictured are check-out girls Sheena Geraghty and Shirley Sutherland, area manager Kenneth McIvor and store manager Donnie Findlay.

A case of "Knees Up, Mother Black" when Seaforth House matron Mrs Cathy Black (left) led her staff in a rousing rendition of traditional songs during the Christmas party at the old folks home in Golspie. Starring with her were (L-R): Alice Sutherland, Lindsay Parkin, Myra Mackay, Jessie Teska, Andrew Macrae and Annie Ross.   1985

The children of Dornoch Playgroup sit in rapt attention at a Punch and Judy show in the West Church Hall, in July 1984.

The Provincial Grand Lodge of Sutherland in April 1977.

Dame Barbra Cartland (above) congratulated the trophy winners at the Loth and Helmsdale annual flower show in 1985 in the community centre, praising them for the quality of their blooms and produce in a most unusually dry growing season.

Sister Sim and Sister Fraser (right) at their farewell party, at the Lawson receiving gifts from nursing officer Mr Richard Starkey. Between the two sisters is Mr Morton Mitchell, Consultant Surgeon.

Singers in Thurso Mod limelight in June 1977:
1) Winners of the John MacDougall Trophy were Durness Primary School.

2) Assynt Youth Choir – Only competitors in their section.

3) Lochinver Primary School Choir with their conductor Mrs Joan Hutchison.

Captain Don Macmillan gets a chairlift from Bunillidh Thistle team mates after they won the PCT Blackhawk North of Scotland 2nd XI in May 1982.

Brora Primary School in 1987 held a very successful Fashion Show, in the assembly hall, and during a break the models posed for a photograph. The ladies are: Isobel Smith, Augustine Sutherland and Liz Dickson. The younger models are back row (L-R): Caroline Thompson, Susan Moodie, Karen Mackay, Louise Port, Faye Pryde, Sally Mackay, and Catherine McGeehan. Middle row: Alison Taylor, Elise Sutherland, Jilly Cole, Jenifer Port, Linda Thom, Emma Maclennan, Debbie Mackay, Shirley Mackay and Jane Mackintosh. Front (standing): Jemma Cole, Susan Macdonald, Yvonne Thom, Leanne Sherick, Carlene Simpson and Colin Simpson. Front row (kneeling): Andrew Wilson, Neil Dunbar, Gavin Thom and Roy Sutherland. Missing from the group are Martin Macleod, Glen Dunbar and Euan Mackay.

This is the Bonar Bridge FC team who have kicked off the new North Reserve League season in great style with two successive wins.

Winners of the Lady Bannerman of Kildonan Cup for their action songs in the Provincial Mod were Lairg Primary School Infants, pictured with their teacher, Mrs Ross.

Many of the 162 members of Sutherland Amateur Swimming Club were there in January 1978 when 12-year-old Malcolm Mackay was presented with the club's Champion Shield. Malcolm, of Fraser Street Golspie, is an asthma sufferer but has swum exceptionally well this year and gained the gold, silver and bronze educational swimming awards. Presenting the shield are the couple who donated it, Golspie pool manager Mr Duncan McInness and his wife Ethel. All the awards are sponsored through the Swimming Teachers Association Ltd, and the shield was given to mark the swimming club's first year. Among those in the photograph are Ann and Philip Martin of Brora who also have gold, silver and bronze awards. (Ann is on the right, in front of her brother, both kneeling).

Four members of the W.R.V.S., all with 20 years service were presented with medals at a recent Inverness rally by the national chairman, Baroness Pike of Melton, Leicestershire. On the left and right of our picture are Mrs Jean Weir, Highland region organiser and Mrs Margaret Maclennan, Sutherland district organiser. In the centre, with Baroness Pike in the middle, are medal winners Mrs Shona Grant, Mrs Margaret King, Mrs Jane Wright and Mrs Isoble Neish.

The Seafaring community of Helmsdale, always generous to the Royal National Lifeboat Institution excelled themselves this year with the magnificent gift of £2000 – representation more than £2 per ever man, woman and child – as a result of their year's efforts. There RNLI branch chairman Billy Cormack hands over the cheque to the grateful Donald Mackay, coxswains of the Wick Lifeboat Princess Marina. Mrs Peggy Innes, the branch president, and this year's 'Lifeboat Queen' Andrena Smith from Brora. Other committee workers and supporters crowded around for the lifeboat visit..

This happy group of lasses at the Durness Games despite the rain, formed into a formidable tug of war team
to represent the home side against Birichen.

Gold Award winners in the Golspie Company of the Junior Boys Brigade in 1987 were presented with their medals by the Rev. Alasdair Maclennan, Minister of Clyne Church of Scotland. And lined up below are the boys who won last year, being presented by former B.B member Mr Neddy Melville with Captain Alan Barclay in attendance. The boys – Now a year older! – are Richard Mackay, Kenneth Hegney, Andrew Colvin, Graham Sutherland, James Dow and Kenneth Melville.

For 12 years Bob Shaw was the popular "lollipop" man at the school crossing patrol outside Dornoch Academy.
On his retiral he was presented with various gifts by his young friends, some of whom are pictured here in 1982.

Some of the prize winners at the highly successful gymkhana held in the Review Park, Dunrobin. Mounted (left – right) – Jan Dunn, Fiona
Low, Jane Cunningham, Steven Ross and Lynne Hedley (youngest rider).

Four Brora girls took the good wishes of the whole of Sutherland with them when they travelled to the Beach Ballroom in Aberdeen to take part in Scottish finals of the National Association of Youth Club's Disco Dancing. Choreographed by Gina Rankine, the quartet – Pamela Brown, Susan Beaumont, Lorna Murray and Lee Rapson – represented the Highland region, and are called Iced Diamond. They were all members of the Brora Youth Club in 1985.

Senior pupils at Golspie High School did their bit for Band Aid Famine Relief campaign when they collected these bags of cereal which were sent to Ethiopia in1985.

Staff at the Lawson Memorial Hospital in 1962.

Pictured in 1983 was the entire company of 40 children, aged from 5-15 years, plus their behind the scenes helpers in the Brora's "Mix 'em and Match 'em" players production of "Goody Two Shoes" in the Brora High School. Produced by Mary Fielding, scored and played by Andrew Betts-Brown, costumed by Lilly Moffat and a team of friends, stage-managed by David Macdonald and Ron Fielding and others, the show was a bright and breezy piece of seasonal relaxation.

Ken Holden of the Sutherland Arms Hotel, Golspie, hands over the 1978 County Singles Darts Championship cup to Angus Ross of Kinbrace, who beat his father, Hugh (second right) in the final. Also pictured are Tony Rettie (Bonar Bridge), who was third and semi-finalist William Bremner, Loth.

These are members of the select darts team who challenged world darts champion John Low of Derby to several exhibition games at the Bunillidh Thistle Social Club in Helmsdale in 1978. John is seated centre of the group, third from the left.

Immediate Past Master Bro Donnie Finlay being invested with regalia by Past Master Bro Bert Macleod at a ceremony at Lodge St Andrew, Golspie. Also pictured are RWM John Mackay, Mrs Nora Findlay and Mrs Agnes Mackay.

Mrs Ella Sutherland, wife of the president of Golspie Bowls Club, A J Sutherland, throws the first jack of the season in 1978.

Andrew Coghill receives a clock and a lamp on his retiral from the Sutherland Estates Sawmill in 1978 after 15 years' service. Handing over the gifts is general manager Jim McLennan. Giving him a good send-off were (left to right): Anthony Campbell, Williams Letters, Victor Ross, James Mackay, Donnie Shaw, George Gunn, George Gore, Joe Polson, Donald Mackay, Donald Gunn, Donald Sutherland and Andrew's son James, who also worked at the sawmill.

Brora Drama Group's A team after their victory at the Sutherland District On-eAct Plays festival at Brora in 1987. Back row – Anne Sutherland, Michael Aitchison (stage manager), Angus Mackenzie, Robert Mackay, Don Sutherland, Tom Aitchison (producer). Seated – Diane Macdonald, Elise Sutherland and Mary Fielding.